Tooth Decay
and Cavities

Dr. Alvin Silverstein,

Virginia Silverstein, and

Laura Silverstein Nunn

My Health

Franklin Watts

A Division of Grolier Publishing

New York • London • Hong Kong • Sydney

Danbury, Connecticut

Special thanks to Dr. Jeffrey Rabinowitz, a partner in Park 56 Dental Group, New York, NY, for allowing photographs to be taken at his office.

Photographs ©: Custom Medical Stock Photo: 17 (Hossler, Ph. D.), 35 right; Peter Arnold Inc.: 19 (Dr. R. Gottsegen), 14 (Alex Grey); Photo Researchers: 16, 21, 23, 30 (Biophoto Associates/SS), 26 (Dr. Jeremy Burgess/SPL), 10 (Doug Martin), 33 (Lawrence Migdale), 31 (Science Pictures Limited/SPL), 35 left (Peter Skinner), 38 (Vision SRI); Randy Matusow: 24, 25, 27, 28; Rigoberto Quinteros: 4, 22; Tony Stone Images: 9 (Gus Butera), 8 (Robert E. Daemmrich); Visuals Unlimited: 11 (Charlie Heidecker), 7 (Joe McDonald), 6 (Science VU).

Medical illustrations by Leonard Morgan
Cartoons by Rick Stromoski

Visit Franklin Watts on the Internet at:
http://publishing.grolier.com

Library of Congress Cataloging-in-Publication Data

Silverstein, Alvin.
    Tooth decay and cavities / by Alvin Silverstein, Virginia Silverstein, and Laura Silverstein Nunn.
        p.   cm.—(My Health)
    Includes bibliographical references and index.
    Summary: Describes the structure and function of teeth and discusses how cavities form and how to prevent them.
    ISBN 0-531-11580-1 (lib. bdg.)   0-531-16412-8 (pbk.)
    1. Dental caries—Juvenile literature.   2. Dental caries in children—Juvenile literature.   [1. Teeth—Care and hygiene.] I. Silverstein, Virginia B. II. Nunn, Laura Silverstein. III. Title. IV. Series.
RK331.S55   1999
617.6′7—dc21
                                                                98-22024
                                                                CIP
                                                                AC

Contents

Teeth for a Lifetime 5

Teeth Tell Tales 6

Two Sets of Teeth 9

Inside Your Mouth 12

What's in a Tooth? 15

The Microworld Inside Your Mouth 17

How Cavities Form 19

Going to the Dentist 24

How to Prevent Cavities 32

Glossary 39

Learning More 43

Index 45

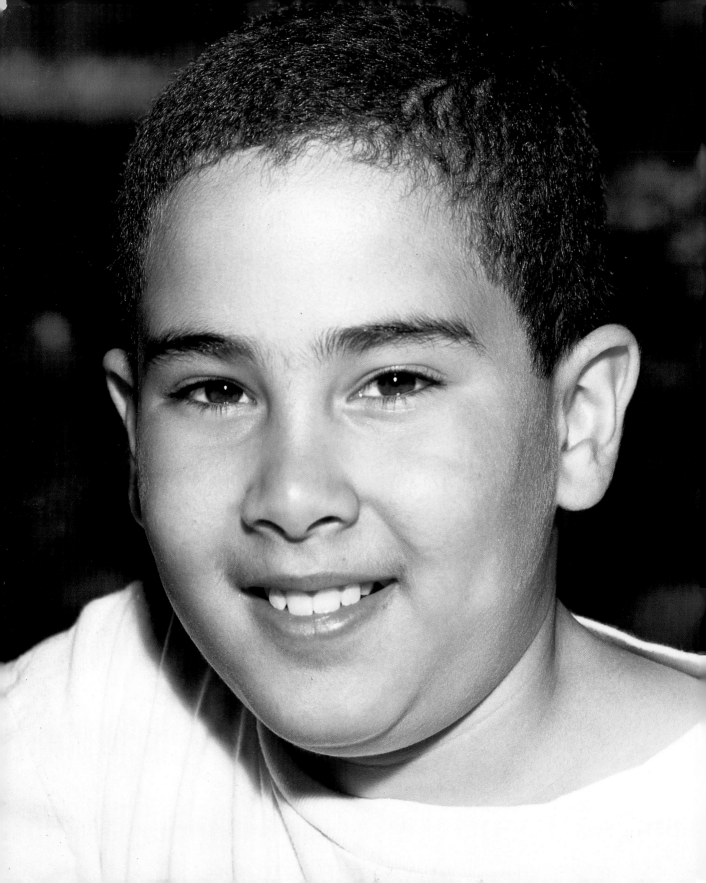

Teeth for a Lifetime

"Say cheese!" That's what people say when they want to take your picture. You give a big, wide smile for the camera to show that you're happy. And when you smile, you show off a nice set of pearly white teeth.

Your teeth aren't there just to make your smile look good. Teeth have a very important job to do—they chew up the food you eat into little pieces so you can swallow it more easily. Actually, you start to digest the food right in your mouth, while you are chewing it.

To help your teeth do their job, you need to take good care of them. If you do, your teeth can last a lifetime.

◄ If you take care of your teeth, you can have a pearly white smile your whole life.

Did You Know...

Some animals, such as birds, lizards, and frogs, do not have teeth. Birds use their strong beaks to tear up food before they swallow it. Lizards and frogs use their long, powerful tongues to snap up food.

Teeth Tell Tales

You can tell a lot about an animal by looking at its teeth. For example, some animals eat only plant foods—leaves, roots, fruits, or seeds. Many plant eaters have very good cutting teeth. Their front teeth are large and sharp so they can snip off leaves and stems or bite off roots with ease. The beaver's front teeth are so big and strong that it can even gnaw through tree trunks. Grazing animals such as horses

Plant eaters, such as this beaver, use their large front teeth to gnaw on branches, stems, and roots.

and cows are plant eaters, too. Their large back teeth are good for grinding up leaves or grains.

Some animals eat mainly meat. They hunt other animals for food. Their teeth are very different from those of plant eaters. Dogs, cats, and other meat eaters have long, pointed fangs. They use them to bite into their prey and tear the meat into pieces small enough to swallow. They have cutting and grinding teeth too, but those teeth are not very big or strong. (If you watch a pet cat or dog eating, you may notice that it does not chew its food very well. It just swallows it down in chunks.)

Meat eaters, such as this gray wolf, use their fangs to tear flesh into pieces small enough to swallow.

Think of all the different types of food on a piece of pizza—cheese, hamburger, pepperoni, mushrooms, onions, peppers, tomatoes. Your teeth can chew them all.

Now look inside your own mouth. Your front teeth are not as strong as a beaver's cutting teeth, but they are good enough to take a bite out of an apple or carrot. Your back teeth are not as big or wide as those of a horse, but you can still crunch vegetables and mash them into a soft pulp. And you don't have long fangs like a cat or a dog, but your teeth can handle meat—even a tough piece of steak—pretty well. People eat both plant foods and meat, so you have teeth that are good for chewing many different types of foods.

Two Sets of Teeth

Babies are born without any teeth at all. At first they can only drink liquids like milk, water, or juice. After a few months, they may eat some soft foods like apple-sauce, ground-up bananas, or mashed peas.

The first teeth, called **milk teeth,** appear when an infant is about 6 months old. One by one they pop

Babies have no teeth.

This 7-year-old girl is missing a front tooth.

out of the **gums**—first the cutting teeth in front, then some grinding teeth and tearing teeth. It takes about 2 years for all 20 milk teeth to come out.

When a child is about 5 or 6 years old, the milk teeth start to fall out. These "baby" teeth are replaced, one at a time, by larger ones called **permanent teeth**. There are 32 teeth in a complete set of permanent teeth. These are the teeth that we keep for the rest of our lives.

Did the Tooth Fairy ever visit your home? In the United States, when you lose a baby tooth, you put it under your pillow. That night, while you are sleeping, the Tooth Fairy takes the tooth, leaving money in its place. In some other countries, children put their baby teeth where a "Tooth Mouse" can find them. They hope their new teeth will be as strong and sharp as a mouse's teeth.

Why do people grow two sets of teeth? A complete set of permanent teeth can't fit into a baby's tiny mouth. That's why they come later, when a child is a little bigger.

Teeth and More Teeth

Animals such as cats and dogs have two sets of teeth, just like people do. Snakes and crocodiles, however, may have several sets of teeth during their lives. And sharks keep on replacing their teeth as long as they live.

A crocodile can replace lost teeth throughout its life.

Inside Your Mouth

You have several kinds of teeth in your mouth. Each type of tooth has a special job to do. When you look in the mirror and smile, you see two rows of flat, squared-off teeth right in the front of your mouth. There are four on top and four smaller teeth below. These front teeth are called **incisors**. They are sharp and act like knives to slice and bite off chunks of food. (Look at your "toothprint" after you bite into an apple to see how broad and sharp your teeth are.)

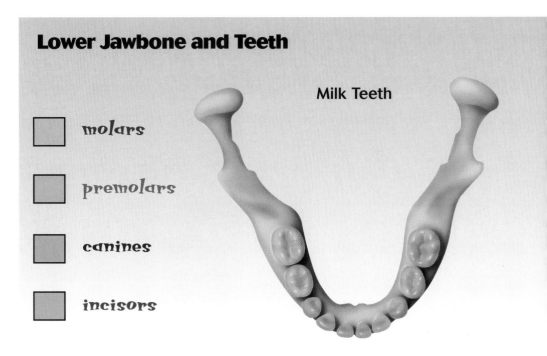

Lower Jawbone and Teeth

Milk Teeth

☐ molars

☐ premolars

☐ canines

☐ incisors

Next to the incisors are teeth called **canines**. The word "canine" comes from the Latin word for "dog." Canine teeth are pointed like the fangs of a dog. We use our canines to tear food into small pieces. You have four canines, two in the upper jaw and two in the lower jaw.

Farther back are the **premolars** and then the **molars**. The premolars have two pointed peaks. They look like two canine teeth put together. The molars are broader and have three pointed peaks. Their tops are flat with raised bumps and ridges. They crush and grind food so that you can swallow it easily.

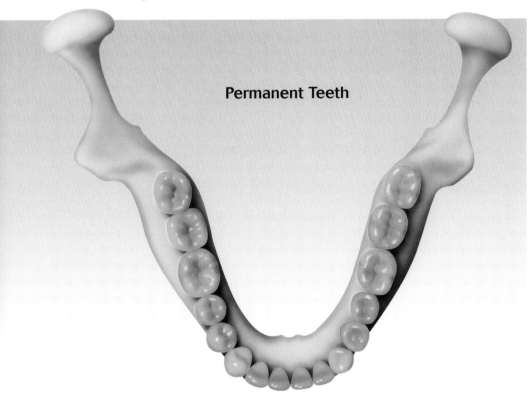

Permanent Teeth

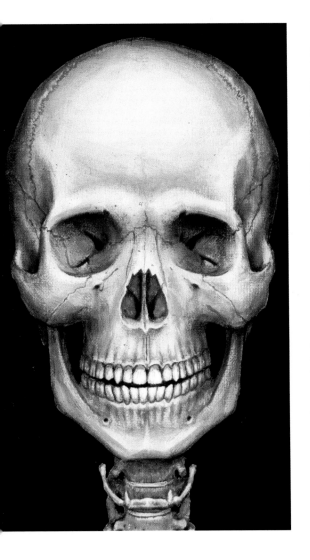

Your teeth are held firmly in place by your **jaws**. Deep inside the upper and lower jaws are **jawbones**. Long roots grow down from each tooth, connecting it to your jawbone. Soft pink gums cover the jawbones and help to hold your teeth in place.

Your upper jawbone cannot move. It is actually a part of your skull, the bony case that forms the shape of your head. Your lower jawbone can move up, down, and even sideways. When you move your jaw, you move your teeth. The muscles that control your jaws are powerful, so your teeth can grind food with great force.

By looking at this human skull, you can see how your teeth are connected to your jawbones.

What's in a Tooth?

What are teeth made of? The whitish covering on the teeth is called **enamel**. It is the hardest substance in your whole body. Only the **crown** of the tooth (the part you can see) and the **neck** (the part at the gum line) are covered with enamel. The **root** is buried deep inside the gum, so it does not need this extra-hard protection.

Under the outer covering of enamel is a hard yellow substance called **dentin**. It is actually harder than bone. Most of the tooth is made up of dentin.

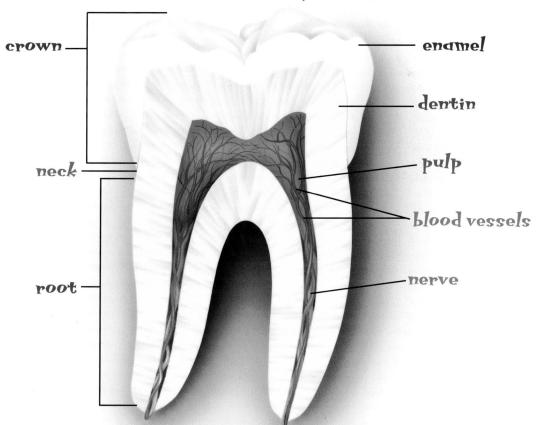

crown

neck

root

enamel

dentin

pulp

blood vessels

nerve

The center of each tooth is filled with soft material called **pulp.** Tiny *blood vessels* and nerves run through the pulp. The blood vessels bring **nutrients** to the dentin and help to keep it healthy and strong. The nerves inside teeth send messages to the brain, so that you always know what your teeth are doing. You can feel it when you bite into something, and know just how hard you are biting.

How White Are Your Teeth?

Toothpaste commercials talk about shining white smiles. But not everyone has bright white teeth. The enamel of some people's teeth is naturally slightly yellow, no matter how much they clean their teeth. In fact, the yellowish enamel may be even stronger than the whiter kind. Stains from foods can also make teeth yellow.

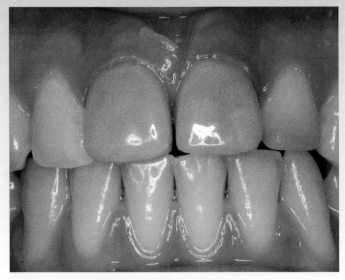

The teeth of adults are sometimes discolored by drinking coffee or tea.

The Microworld Inside Your Mouth

Would you believe that there are millions of tiny creatures living inside your body? These creatures, known as **bacteria,** are so small that you need a microscope to see them.

Many kinds of bacteria live in our bodies. Some are "good," and some are "bad." "Good" bacteria help us. For instance, the bacteria that live in your intestines break down the food you eat so that you can **digest** it more easily. "Bad" bacteria hurt us. Some bacteria make us sick. For instance, you get strep throat because bacteria attack your body and make you ill.

If you could look at your teeth through a microscope, this is what you'd see.

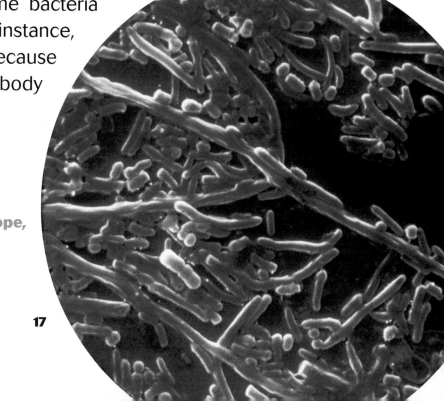

17

If you could look through a microscope at the inside of your own mouth, you might be shocked at what you saw. A tiny world of bacteria is having a party inside your mouth! At this party, you bring the food and the bacteria just eat. When you eat a hamburger, for example, you chew it up into tiny pieces with your teeth, and then you swallow it. Now the hamburger is all gone, right? Well, not exactly. Every time you eat something, tiny bits of food are left on your teeth. Bacteria feed on these little bits of food. And these bacteria are germs that can really harm your teeth.

Did You Know...

Bacteria are not the only things living inside your mouth. Other tiny creatures, called **tooth amoebas,** live there too. They are very much like the amoebas that live in ponds. Under a microscope, they look like shapeless blobs of jelly. Tooth amoebas help to protect your teeth by feeding on bacteria, as well as on the bits of food left in your teeth.

How Cavities Form

Millions of bacteria feast on the food left in your teeth. Bacteria grow and multiply, eventually covering your teeth with a soft, sticky coat of **plaque.** Plaque is a mixture of bits of leftover food, bacteria, and other substances. It forms mainly between the teeth and at the edge of the gums. When you do not clean your teeth regularly, plaque can build up. If left for more than a few days, plaque hardens into **tartar,** which is more difficult to remove.

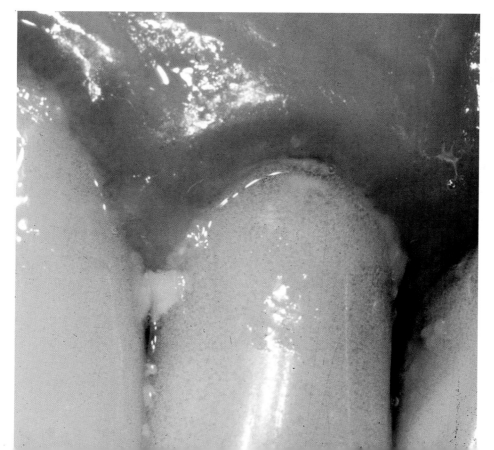

As you can see in this picture, plaque often builds up where the teeth meet the gums.

As bacteria grow on your teeth, they make an acid that slowly eats through the tooth enamel. This is **tooth decay**. And once it gets through the hard enamel into the softer dentin, that acid works fast. Eventually, tooth decay makes a **cavity**—a hole in the tooth. Bacteria make even more acid when you eat sugary foods. That's why people say, "Don't eat so much candy—it will rot your teeth."

Activity 1: How Is an Egg Like a Tooth?

You can try to make an eggshell decay, just like a tooth. You'll need a hard-boiled egg (cooked by an adult) and a bowl of vinegar. Let the egg sit in the vinegar for about a day. Vinegar is acidic, just like the acid that the bacteria make in your mouth. When you check on the egg, you'll see that part of the shell has been eaten away by the vinegar. Tooth decay works the same way.

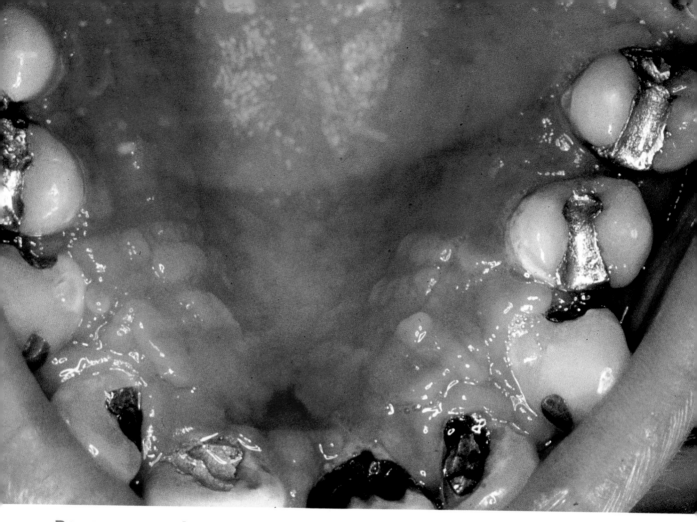

Do your parents have a mouth full of fillings? If they do, you might too one day. Even so, brushing with fluoride toothpaste and flossing can help you have a healthier mouth.

You may get cavities when you are older—no matter how well you take care of your teeth. Studies show that good or bad teeth may be **inherited.** So you could have nice strong teeth like your mom—or get a mouth full of cavities like your dad.

Ice cream cones are usually a treat. But if you have a cavity, eating one can be painful.

Your teeth may give you some clues to let you know that a cavity is forming. If eating hot soup or a cold ice cream cone makes your teeth hurt, you may have a cavity.

When acid from bacteria eats away the tooth enamel and then the dentin, it moves into the pulp. As soon as it comes into contact with a nerve—ouch! You have a toothache. Toothaches can be very painful and should be checked by a dentist. But not all toothaches are that serious. Sometimes, food gets stuck between

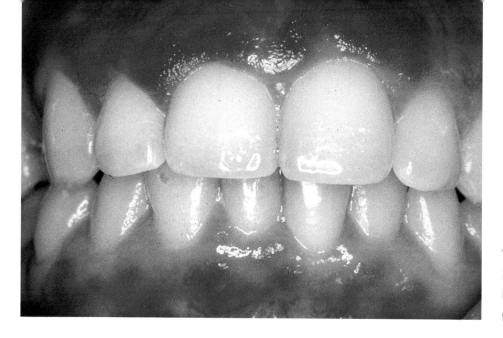

This person has a very bad case of gingivitis.

teeth. This can bother your gums, and cause your tooth to throb with pain. The good news is that you can avoid this pain by making sure your teeth stay clean.

Bacteria can also grow down into the gums and cause **gum disease.** Gum disease usually affects adults. One of the most common types of gum disease is **gingivitis,** or swelling of the gums.

Your body does not let bacteria take over your mouth without a fight. It has a defense called **saliva**— the watery stuff that fills your mouth when you eat, or sometimes even when you think about food. Saliva mixes with your food to make chewing and swallowing easier. Saliva also helps to clean your teeth by washing away food leftovers. It contains substances that help cut down the amount of acid made by the bacteria.

Going to the Dentist

How often do you go to the dentist? You should have a checkup every 6 months. That is the best way to keep from getting cavities.

In a routine visit, the dentist first checks all your teeth, looking for any problems. Holes or cracks in the enamel and dark-colored spots on the teeth are signs of trouble. But sometimes cavities are hard to spot,

This dentist is checking a boy's teeth for cavities.

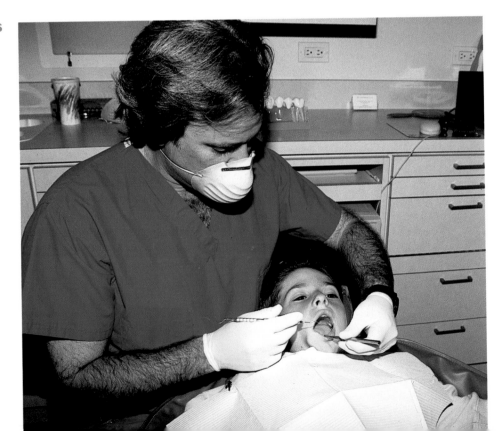

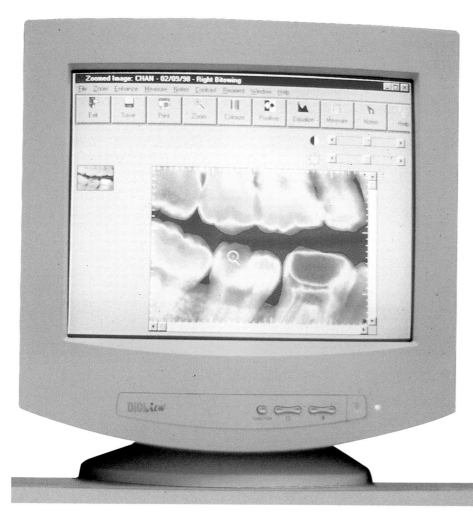

Zoomed Image: CHAN - 02/09/98 - Right Bitewing

The red area on this computer-enhanced view of an X ray shows a cavity.

especially if they are between teeth or at the edge of the gums.

The dentist can find those cavities by taking X-ray pictures of your teeth. X rays show parts of the teeth and jawbone that are hidden inside the gums. If you are lucky, the X rays will show that you do not have any cavities. But if you do have cavities, the X rays will show the dentist exactly where they are.

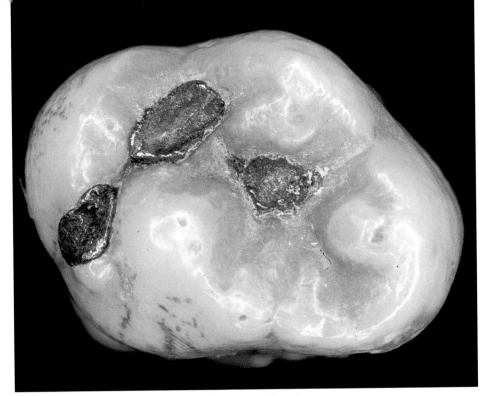

This molar has three amalgam fillings.

Cavities should be fixed as soon as possible so that the tooth decay does not get any worse. To do this, the dentist must put a **filling** in the cavity. Most fillings are made of **amalgam,** a mixture of silver and other metals. But if the cavity is in a tooth that shows when you smile, the dentist may use a mixture of tooth-colored materials called **porcelain.**

The dentist can't just put the filling right into the cavity. Bits of food and bacteria might be hiding there. If they are not removed, the bacteria might continue to grow and multiply, producing more acid and making a bigger hole in your tooth. Dentists use a drill to clean out the hole and get rid of all the bad stuff. (Before the dentist starts to drill, you may be given a shot, or a patch with a pain-killing drug may be placed on your gum. This numbs your mouth so you will not feel any pain.

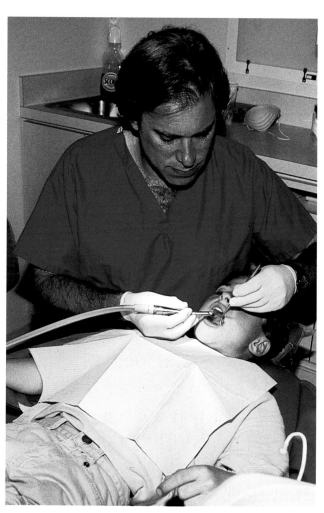

A dentist is drilling a patient's tooth before filling a cavity.

High-Tech Tools

If a cavity is small, today's dentists can use some painless new tools instead of drilling. They may clean out the cavity with a high-speed jet of air. Or they may use a **laser drill**—a pinpoint beam of laser light combined with water—to cool and clean a cavity. Lasers can also be used to remove plaque or to treat gum disease by killing bacteria between the teeth and gums. Some dentists use laser light with a bleaching mixture to make teeth whiter.

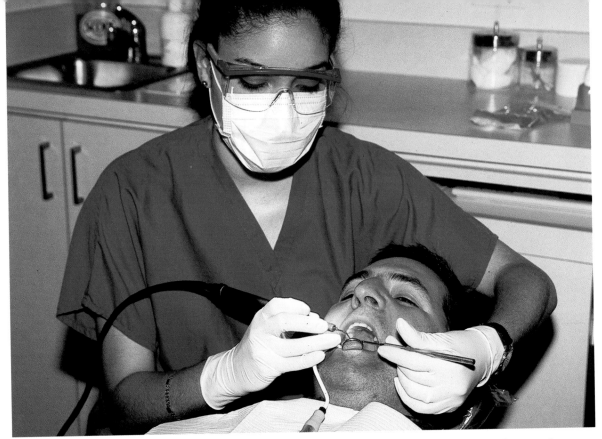

This dental hygienist is scraping tartar off a man's teeth.

When a cavity has been cleaned out and shaped, the dentist packs in the filling material. After it dries and hardens, the filling may need a little drilling and polishing to make it just the right shape to fit with your other teeth when you chew.

After the dentist has examined your teeth and fixed any cavities, it is time for a cleaning that will leave your teeth smooth and healthy. The dentist (or dental hygienist) may use a special tool called a probe to remove any bits of food stuck between your teeth.

Other metal tools may be used to scrape away the plaque that has built up. Or the dentist may use a device that blasts away the plaque with a beam of **ultrasound.** Finally, an electric toothbrush cleans and polishes your teeth. (The dentist may let you choose the flavor of the toothpaste—how about strawberry, orange, cinnamon, or even chocolate?)

Sometimes a tooth is so badly decayed that it can't be saved. In that case, the dentist may have to **extract,** or pull out, the tooth. Usually you will be given **anesthesia** for a tooth extraction, to keep you from feeling any pain. After the tooth is taken out, your gum may feel sore for a while.

Sometimes a badly damaged tooth can be saved by **root canal therapy.** A root canal is a narrow, hollow tunnel in a tooth's root. When the decay spreads down into the tooth, the pulp may become infected. Then a dentist may treat the infection by performing

Early Dentists

Hundreds of years ago, people did not have dentists. There were only "tooth pullers." These tooth pullers had different methods for pulling teeth. Some tied a string to the patient's tooth and pulled. Others used a tool to yank teeth out. Sometimes tooth pullers hired musicians to play loud music so that people in the neighborhood wouldn't be frightened by a patient's screams.

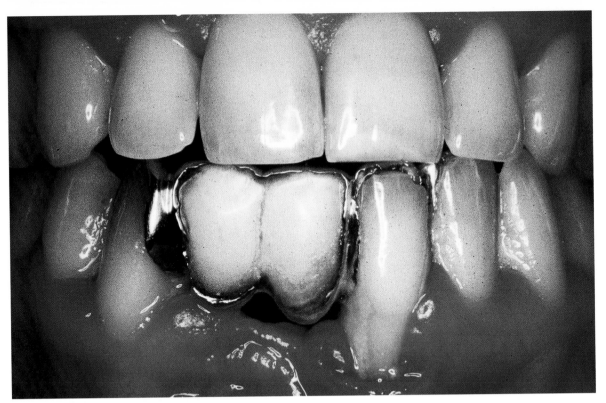

This metal bridge connects two false teeth to healthy teeth on either side of the hole.

root canal therapy to take out the pulp. The pulp is replaced with a solid packing material that helps to hold the tooth in place.

When accidents happen, a tooth may be chipped, broken, or cracked. As long as the root of the tooth is not damaged, it can probably be saved. One way is by putting a crown, or cap, on it. The crown is cemented right over the damaged tooth. It can look as good and work as well as a normal tooth. If the whole tooth is missing, the dentist may make a **bridge.** This is a false tooth that is attached to good teeth on either

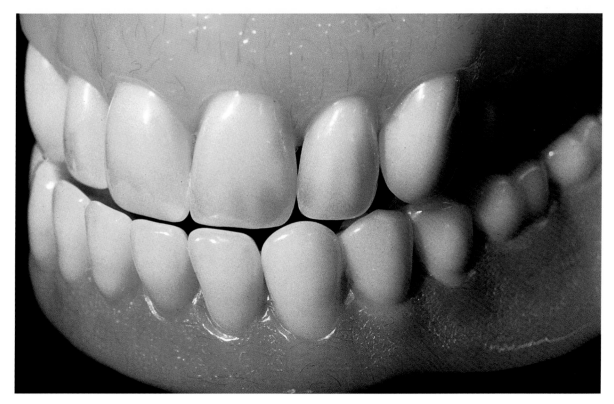

The false teeth in a denture rest in a tough, plastic base that is fitted to the patient's mouth.

side of the empty space. A missing tooth can also be replaced with an **implant**—a false tooth that is set into the gum and permanently attached to the jaw-bone. Implants work like natural teeth. If all of the teeth are missing or have to be taken out, the dentist can make a complete set of false teeth, which is called a **denture.**

Dentists have many ways to fix teeth, but they'd much rather find no cavities at all when you come in for a checkup. You can help the dentist take care of your teeth by brushing and flossing them regularly at home.

How to Prevent Cavities

Brushing and flossing your teeth and gums makes a big difference in preventing tooth decay. Cleaning your teeth does not have to be a chore. If you do it every day, brushing and flossing becomes a habit, just like taking a shower or combing your hair.

Are Your Teeth Clean?

With your fingernail, scrape very gently along some of your teeth, starting at the gums. Did you scrape off some soft, whitish stuff? That is plaque.

Be sure to use a toothpaste with **fluoride** in it. Fluoride helps protect your teeth from tooth decay by making the enamel even stronger.

Many cities now add fluoride to their drinking water. Thanks to fluoride, children today get only 36 percent as many cavities as children did 40 years ago. The American Dental Association advises that fluoridated water, fluoridated toothpaste, and fluoridated mouthwash are great ways to fight tooth decay.

You should brush your teeth after every meal, but that's not always easy—especially if you like to have snacks during the day. Be sure to brush your teeth at least twice a day—when you get up in the morning and before you go to bed. Researchers found that if teeth are cleaned at least once within 24 hours, bacteria cannot make enough acid to damage them.

Brush at least twice a day to keep your teeth healthy.

How to Brush Your Teeth

How do you brush your teeth? Here are some general rules for a complete cleaning:

1. Move your toothbrush up and down and in circles.

2. Brush the top teeth downward from the gums.

3. Brush the bottom teeth upward from the gums.

4. Brush the backs of the top and bottom teeth.

5. Remember to brush the top and bottom rows of your teeth, too. Also, brush the flat surfaces and the sides of these teeth.

6. Rinse thoroughly—and smile.

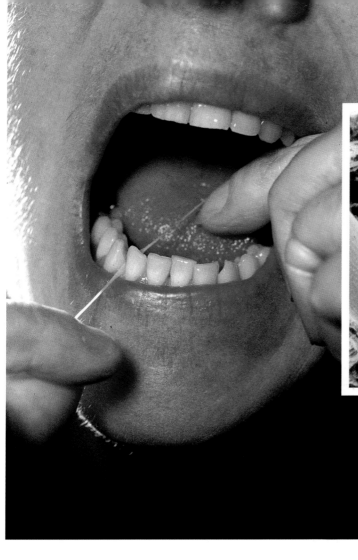

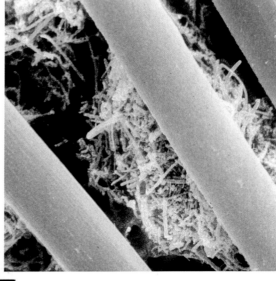

▲ A picture taken through a microscope can show bacteria on a piece of dental floss.

◄ Flossing can remove the bacteria and food particles that brushing misses.

You should get a new toothbrush every 2 to 3 months. Bacteria can grow in a toothbrush, so you put germs into your mouth when you use it.

You should also floss at least once a day. Bacteria feed on food that is left between your teeth. Moving a strand of dental floss back and forth between your teeth will remove the bits of food you missed while you were brushing.

Activity 2: How Clean Are Your Teeth?

You can find out by using disclosing tablets or a special mouthwash that colors the plaque on your teeth with a bright vegetable dye. You can buy the tablets from the drugstore, or your dentist may give you some samples.

Chew a tablet for 30 seconds but do not swallow it. Wash your mouth out with water and look in a mirror. Where are the darkest plaque stains? These places show you where you need to brush your teeth better next time.

What kinds of foods do you eat? Do you eat a lot of vegetables and fruits? What about candy? We're told to stay away from sweets like cookies and candy. But you might be surprised to learn that foods like cornflakes and raisins may be to blame for the holes in your teeth. Starches like potato chips and crackers may not taste sweet, but to bacteria, they're just like lollipops. Saliva breaks starches down into a sugar called maltose, and bacteria really love maltose. Starches are especially bad for your teeth because they actually stick around longer than sugars do. This gives bacteria more time to cause cavities.

You probably have heard the popular saying in milk commercials: "Milk does a body good." It's true. Milk, cheese, and green vegetables contain **calcium,** which helps keep your bones and teeth strong and healthy. Other substances in these foods are also good for your teeth.

Foods that Stick

Barely Sticky	Moderately Sticky	Very Sticky
Apples	White bread	Granola bars
Bananas	Caramels	Oatmeal cookies
Hot fudge sundaes	Cream-filled sponge cakes	Potato chips
Chocolate candy bars		Salted crackers
		Raisins
		Cream-filled sandwich cookies
		Peanut butter crackers

Have Some Cheese Please!

Have a piece of cheddar cheese for a snack. Cheese somehow increases the amount of saliva that flows in your mouth. As you know, saliva decreases the amount of acid that is produced by bacteria. So, when you eat cheese, you are actually helping to protect your teeth.

Cheese is a good source of calcium. It also increases the amount of saliva in your mouth.

If you watch what you eat and brush and floss your teeth after meals, you will help make your teeth the best that they can be.

Would you believe that there could be a vaccine for tooth decay by the year 2000? That's what some researchers say. In addition, dentists are finding better methods to identify people who are more likely to have tooth decay. This means that young children will have an even better chance to keep their teeth healthy and strong all their lives.

Glossary

amalgam—a mixture of silver and other metals used for filling cavities.

anesthesia—a drug used to stop a person from feeling pain.

bacteria—tiny living things that are too small to see without a microscope.

blood vessel—one of the tubes that carries blood throughout the body.

bridge—one or more false teeth used to replace a missing tooth or teeth. It is attached to the good teeth on each side of the empty space.

calcium—a chemical element found in teeth and bones.

canines—pointed teeth on each side of the incisors. They are used to tear food.

cavity—a hole in a tooth, produced by tooth decay.

crown—the top part of a tooth, above the gums. It can also refer to an artificial cap placed over a broken or damaged tooth.

dentin—a hard, yellowish substance that makes up most of a tooth.

denture—a complete set of false teeth that can be removed from the mouth.

digest—to break down food so that it can be used by the body.

enamel—the outer covering of a tooth; the hardest material in the body.

extract—to pull out a tooth.

filling—a substance that a dentist puts into a cavity to stop tooth decay.

fluoride—a mineral that helps to make teeth stronger. It may be added to toothpaste or drinking water or applied to the teeth by a dentist.

gingivitis—inflammation (painful swelling) of the gums.

gum disease—damage to the gums caused by trapped food or bacteria.

gums—the soft pink tissue inside the mouth that surrounds the teeth.

implant—a false tooth that is set into the gum and permanently attached to the jawbone.

incisors—front teeth with flat, squared-off shape. These teeth are used for cutting.

inherited—passed from parent to child.

jawbones—the bones of the upper and lower jaws, to which the roots of the teeth are attached. Only the lower jawbone can move.

jaws—bony structures between the nose and the chin that hold the teeth.

laser drill—a pinpoint-sized beam of laser light that is combined with water and used to clean out cavities before filling them.

milk teeth—a child's first set of teeth.

molars—broad teeth with three points, the farthest back in the mouth. They crush and grind food.

neck—the middle part of a tooth, at the gum line.

nerve—a structure that carries messages to the brain

nutrients—vitamins and minerals needed for good health.

permanent teeth—teeth that replace the milk teeth.

plaque—a mixture of leftover food, bacteria, and other substances that forms on teeth, especially between teeth and at the edge of the gums.

porcelain—a hard, tooth-colored substance used for filling cavities.

premolars—teeth with two points, on each side of the canines. They can tear and grind food.

pulp—a soft substance that fills the center of a tooth. It contains nerves and blood vessels.

root—the lower part of a tooth, which holds it in the gums and attaches it to the jawbone.

root canal therapy—replacement of the pulp in the root of an infected tooth with solid packing material.

saliva—the watery fluid that forms in the mouth and helps in chewing and swallowing food.

tartar—another name for plaque; plaque that has been hardened by calcium deposits

tooth amoeba—a microscopic jelly-like creature that lives in the gums and feeds on bacteria.

tooth decay—the effects of acid, produced by bacteria in the mouth, which eats through the outer layers of a tooth, producing a hole or cavity.

ultrasound—very high-pitched sound used in a tool for cleaning teeth.

Learning More

Books

Bridget and Neil Ardley, *Skin, Hair, and Teeth*. Englewood Cliffs,
   NJ: Silver Burdett, 1988.

Roger Diévart, *Teeth, Tusks and Fangs*. Ossining, NY: Young
   Discovery Library, 1991.

Jennifer Storey Gillis, *Tooth Truth: Fun Facts & Projects*.
   Pownal, VT: Storey Communications, 1996.

Organizations and Online Sites

Academy of General Dentistry
211 East Chicago Ave., Suite 1200
Chicago, IL 60611-2670
http://www.agd.org/consumer

American Dental Association
211 East Chicago Ave.
Chicago, IL 60611
E-mail: online@ada.org
http://www.ada.org/tc-cons.html
ADA "Kids' Corner" with coloring sheets and movies
http://www.ada.org/consumer/kids/index.html

The Dental Consumer Advisor
http://www.toothinfo.com/
This site has a variety of useful information.

Dental Health Fact Sheets
http://www.pe.net/~iddpc1/facts.htm
This has all kinds of interesting information about teeth and keeping them healthy.

Lessons for a Lifetime of Healthy Smiles
http://www.floridadental.org/fda/dentallines/teaching
This site explains how to care for your teeth.

Organized Dentistry Associations
http://www.dental-resources.com/assoc2.html
This site can help you find a dentist in your area.

Tooth Fairy Links to Fun and Dental Health
http://members.tripod.com/~toothfairytales/
This site has a variety of links to fun facts, activities, songs, and products.

Index

Page numbers in *italics* indicate illustrations.

Activities
  how clean are your teeth?, 36
  make an eggshell decay, 20
Amalgam fillings, 26, *26*
Anesthesia, 29
Animals
  grazing, 6–7
  meat eaters, 7, *7*
  plant eaters, 6–7, *6*
  without teeth, 5, *5*

Babies, 9, *9*
Baby teeth. *See* Milk teeth
Bacteria, 17–18, *17*, 19–23,
  36–37
    and brushing, 33, 35
    and flossing, 35, *35*

and gum disease, 23, *23*, 27
    and saliva, 23, 38
    and tooth amoebas, 18Blood
vessels, *15*, 16
Bridge, 30–31, *30*
Brushing, 31, 32–34, *33*, 38
  how to brush, 34

Canines (teeth), *12*, 12
Cap, 30
Cavities
  finding, 24–25, *24*, *25*
  fixing, 26–27, *26*, *27*
  how they form, 19–23, *19*, *21*,
    22
  preventing, 24, 32–38, *33*,
    35, *38*
Chewing, 5, 7, 8, *8*, 23
Cleaning teeth, 28–29, *28*, 32
  testing for plaque, 32, 36
Color of teeth, 16, *16*
  pearly white teeth, *4*, 5
  whitening with laser, 27
Crown
  artificial cap, 30
  top part of tooth, 15, *15*
Cutting teeth, 6, *6*, 7, 8, 10

Dental hygienist, 28, *28*
Dentin, 15, *15*, 16, 20
Dentist, 24–25, *24*
Denture, 31, *31*
Drilling, 26–27, *27*, 28

Eggshell, make it decay, 20
Enamel, 15, *15*
  color of, 16, *16*
  signs of trouble, 24
  strengthened by fluoride, 32
  and tooth decay, 20
Extracting teeth, 29

False teeth, 30–31, *30, 31*
Fangs, 7, *7*, 13
Fillings, *21*, 26, *26*, 28
First teeth. *See* Milk teeth
Flossing, *21*, 31, 32, 35, *35*, 38
Fluoride, *21*, 32
Flossing
  removing with a probe, 28
  and saliva, 23
  stains from, 16, *16*
  sugary, 20
  and tooth amoebas, 18

Germs. *See* Bacteria
Gingivitis, 23, *23*
Grazing animals, 6–7
Grinding, 7, 13, 14

Gums, 10, 14
  and extracting teeth, 29
  gum disease, 23, *23*, 27
  and plaque, 19, *19*

Implant, 31
Incisors, 12, *12*
Inheritance and teeth, 21

Jawbones, *12–13*, 14, *14*, 25
  implants, 31
Jaws, 14

Kinds of teeth, 12–13
  canines, *12*, 13
  incisors, 12, *12*
  milk teeth, 9–10, 11, *12*
  molars, *12*, 13, *26*
  permanent teeth, 10, 11, *13*
  premolars, *12*, 13

Laser drill, 27
Losing teeth. *See also*
  Extracting teeth
    milk teeth, 10, *10*, 11

Meat eaters, 7, *7*, 8, *8*
Milk, 37
Milk teeth, 9–10, *12*
  and the Tooth Fairy, 11
Molars, *12*, 13, *26*

Neck, 15, *15*
Nerve, *15*, 16
Number of permanent teeth, 10

Pain, 22–23, *22*
  and anesthesia, 29
  and drilling, 27, *27*
  and temperature, 22, *22*
Pearly white teeth, *4*, 5
Permanent teeth, 10, 11, *13*
Plant eaters, 6–7, *6*
Plaque, 19, *19*
  removing, 27, 29
  testing for, 32, 36
Porcelain, 26
Premolars, *12*, 13
Pulling teeth, 29
Pulp, *15*, 16, 22
  removing, 29–30

Root, 15, *15*, 30
Root canal, 29
Root canal therapy, 29–30

Saliva, 23, 36–37
  and cheese, 38, *38*

Skull (human), 14, *14*
Starches, 36–37
Sticky foods, 37
Sugary foods, 20, 36, 37

Tartar, 19, *28*
Teeth
  what they do, 5
  what they're made of, 15–16,
    15
Toothache, 22–23
Tooth amoebas, 18
Toothbrush, electric, 29
Tooth decay, 20
  preventing, 32
  vaccine for, 38
Tooth Fairy, 11

Ultrasound, 29

Vaccine for tooth decay, 38

X rays of teeth, 25, *25*

About the Authors

Dr. Alvin Silverstein is a Professor of Biology at the College of Staten Island of the City University of New York. **Virginia Silverstein** is a translator of Russian scientific literature. The Silversteins first worked together on a research project at the University of Pennsylvania. Since then, they have produced six children and more than 150 published books for young people.

Laura Silverstein Nunn, a graduate of Kean College, has been helping with her parents' books since her high-school days. She is the coauthor of more than twenty books on diseases and health, science concepts, endangered species, and pets. Laura lives with her husband Matt and their young son Cory in a rural New Jersey town not far from her childhood home.